©2008-2010 Periscope Film LLC
All Rights Reserved
www.PeriscopeFilm.com

ISBN # 978-1-935700-00-5

HEISLER
GEARED LOCOMOTIVES

PRINTED
IN
U.S.A.

"We're hauling *more*
at lower cost
with our HEISLER Locomotives"

ALL through this book you'll see reports from HEISLER users that give an idea of the *extra profits* produced by this modern locomotive.

These reports have come in from many different industries.

Nearly all owners have been able to move 35% to 50% more material with their HEISLERS, than with the locomotives previously used. These improvements have been shown on rough track with grades and sharp curves, as well as on smooth track with easy grades.

When you read the following pages, and see the reports and photos of locomotives that have given such results, you'll understand why men who have "tried them all" have rated the HEISLER as *unequalled for heavy hauling*.

And you'll also see why we can put the HEISLER on your work with the *definite guarantee* to haul at least 30% more, ton per ton of locomotive.

Where to find the facts you want:

HEISLER
GEARED LOCOMOTIVES

PRINTED IN U.S.A.

One of five HEISLERS used by the Lehigh Navigation Coal Company on their Summit Hill stripping, near Lansford, Pa. The report printed at left tells how these HEISLERS have given greater hauling capacity, and lower hauling costs.

Outhauling its guarantee by a good margin

The photo above shows one of the 55-ton HEISLERS used on the Lehigh Navigation Coal Co's., Summit Hill stripping near Lansford, Pa.

On a 3% grade, this HEISLER easily starts and hauls four 30-yard cars weighing 80 to 90 tons each. The same locomotive starts and hauls three 30-yard cars on a 4½% grade with a 25 degree curve— which is of course considerably above its guaranteed hauling capacity.

A 36-ton HEISLER of the Atlantic Gypsum Products Company, hauling gypsum cars out of the quarry at Cheticamp, Nova Scotia.

One of 6 HEISLERS on the largest stripping in the world— at the new United Electric Fidelity Mine. Note the big Marion "5600" shovel in the background. On all of the HEISLER-equipped United Electric operations, two HEISLERS per unit are used, additional locomotives being unnecessary.

Why users rate the HEISLER as
"unequalled for low-cost hauling"

The strong endorsements that you'll read throughout this book are easily understood, when you size up the modern HEISLER'S design and construction.

Here's a modern locomotive that is built especially for heavy hauling— *built to meet the actual conditions found in strip mines, quarries, logging operations, gravel pits, and general industrial hauling.*

HEISLER users tell you that this locomotive has no equal for heavy hauling and switching, because it has—

(1) *More hauling power*, 30% to 50% more than an ordinary locomotive of same weight— or even better.

The HEISLER'S engine pistons deliver 2 to 2½ times as many power impulses per revolution of the drivers, giving a much higher starting torque, uniformly applied. This smoother flow of power is *put to work*, as every wheel is a driver. The HEISLER starts its heavier loads with practically no slipping or jerking.

(2) *Plenty of speed.* On switching and spotting of cars you'll find that the HEISLER is 20% to 25% faster than a steam rod engine of the same weight. In comparison with gasoline locomotives, the HEISLER has given users considerably greater speed. On your longer hauls the HEISLER can be run at the highest speed at which you're able to haul your cars.

(3) *Much better flexibility* for hauling over rough temporary track, with sharp curves and grades. The HEISLER'S patented truck construction keeps every

This 36-ton HEISLER easily starts 18 cars of gypsum, weighing 324 tons, on a 2.1 grade with a 7 degree curve. On the same haul a 32-ton rod engine hauls only eight cars. The HEISLER makes better time with its bigger load than the rod engine, over the 2½-mile run from quarry to crusher.

wheel in constant contact with the rail, even on the roughest kind of track.

(4) *Operating and maintenance costs are lower.* Because of the HEISLER'S more efficient engine speed, resulting in improved combustion and fuel economy, many operators are reporting 25% to 30% savings in fuel cost per ton-mile. Engine upkeep is lower because the flexible construction of the HEISLER does not allow shocks and strains due to rough track to be transmitted to the driving mechanism, cylinders, valve gear, main frame and boiler. The truck construction of the HEISLER has a cushioning effect that is not unlike the comparison between a heavy truck with pneumatic tires and one with solid tires.

(5) *Dependable service* is assured by the HEISLER'S simple, rugged construction. It stands up to the hardest work, continuously. Let us send you reports from owners, showing how they have found the HEISLER for *Reliability*.

Big Capacity— Speed— Flexibility— Economy— Reliability— this is the combination that has produced *extra profits* on every class of hauling.

Past performance has made it possible for us to put a HEISLER Locomotive on your work with the *definite guarantee* to haul at least 30% more material, ton per ton of locomotive, while hauling at the speed you require.

Read what these important advantages of the HEISLER have meant to users in many industries.

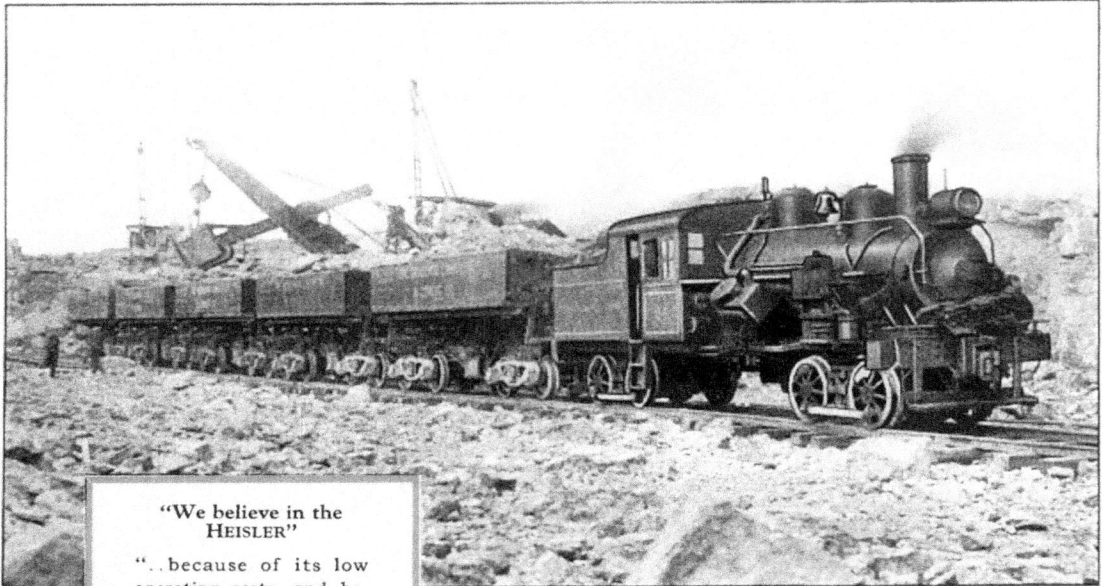

A 50-ton HEISLER, easily hauling five loaded 25-yard cars over varying grades from quarry to crusher, for the Bessemer Limestone and Cement Company, Youngstown, Ohio.

"We believe in the HEISLER"

"..because of its low operating costs, and because it moves the greatest volume of material in a single trip over grades up to 3%, and does it easily."
—Bessemer Limestone & Cement Co., Youngstown, Ohio.

On this particular haul the rod engine pulled 8 loaded dump cars— and the HEISLER, with cars of exactly the same weight, loaded the same way, on exactly the same trip, is hauling 15. (Name on request).

Class 90 HEISLER, weighing 110 tons working order, on the Rainier, Wash., operation of the Weyerhaeuser Timber Company. The locomotive regularly hauls 15 cars of logs, weighing 632 tons on 3% grade. Rated capacity of this engine is 542 tons on this grade. The HEISLER also hauls 15 empties, weighing 210 tons, to the woods against 6% grades and 34 degree curves. This is one of 10 HEISLERS used on various Weyerhaeuser Timber Company's operations.

HEISLER
GEARED LOCOMOTIVES

Reasons for Greater *Hauling* Power that makes the HEISLER superior to other locomotives for heavy hauling

Your inspection of the HEISLER'S design will explain why the HEISLER makes good on the strong guarantee behind it — and often does considerably better.

It is not at all unusual for a HEISLER to show as high as 60% to 100% increase in hauling capacity, over a rod engine and tender of the same weight, without sacrifice of speed.

The HEISLER has one big advantage in its *very much higher starting torque.* Its engine pistons make 2 to 2½ times as many power impulses as a rod engine's, per revolution of the driving wheels, giving a much smoother flow of power. It's like comparing an 8-cylinder motor car with a 4-cylinder.

This is one reason why the HEISLER starts a heavy load more easily than a rod engine of the same weight, and about 20% to 25% faster — making a corresponding gain in hauling time.

Besides, power losses through friction are cut to the minimum, as the HEISLER'S power is transmitted direct from its central crankshaft to the driving axles.

All of the HEISLER'S extra power is *put to work* in hauling

The greater power that is developed by the HEISLER'S V-type engines is *actually delivered* when pulling a train.

When you watch a HEISLER pulling its heavier loads, you'll note that the drivers do not have the same tendency as a rod engine's to slip on the track.

Every one of the wheels is a driver, regard-less of the size HEISLER you are using. No idling wheels — and every pound of the locomotive's weight is utilized to give the drivers a better grip on the track — a most important factor in hauling capacity.

The two-truck HEISLERS with their weight distributed on 8 driving wheels have double the rail contact of a 0-4-0 type rod engine. And at least 50% more rail contact than a six-wheel type switcher. The three largest HEISLERS, with their weight distributed on 3 swiveling trucks of 4 drivers each, have a correspondingly increased contact. On rough track there is even a greater increase in rail contact because of the flexibility of HEISLER truck construction which gives uniform traction for every driving wheel regardless of track conditions.

Because of the HEISLER'S smoother flow of power — its greater rail contact — its 100% utilization of weight — the HEISLER shows a very valuable increase in hauling power even when you are hauling over the smoothest well-ballasted track, with practically no grades or sharp curves.

One of the four 42-ton HEISLERS at the West Clinton, Indiana, operation of the Electric Shovel Coal Corporation. These locomotives have a long haul from pit to tipple and must overcome fairly stiff grades coming out of the pits.

Hundreds of HEISLERS have shown splendid economies under these conditions.

For straight, level inter-plant runs, the HEISLER has all the speed you can use — and its greater hauling power is there whenever needed.

And when you have to haul over rough track, with sharp curves and grades, the HEISLER shows even greater increases in hauling capacity.

The president of a
coal company writes
to another operator:

"We have a very hard
grade of 6% to 7%, up
which we could handle 7 or
8 cars with two 18-ton rod
engines, one pushing and
one pulling. Our 32-ton
HEISLER now takes 12
to 15 cars up this grade
with ease, releasing two
rod engines from service.
The HEISLER is a very
fine investment."—(Name
on request).

This 42-ton HEISLER— hauling
five 43-ton capacity coal cars—is
one of 10 HEISLERS operated by
the Electric Shovel Coal Corporation on their various operations.

On this haul a 50-ton HEISLER
handles three cars with much
greater ease than the 63-ton saddle
tank. (Name and details on
request).

This 50-ton HEISLER is "moving more material per trip and
doing it easily," for an Eastern
quarry operator.

HEISLER
GEARED LOCOMOTIVES

Reports from users show that the HEISLER *consistently* makes good on its guarantee

The records printed in this book, and many others that we can send you, show clearly that you can put the HEISLER on your work and be *definitely sure* of increasing your hauled tonnage at least 30% per ton of locomotive.

And in many cases the HEISLER outhauls a rod engine of the same weight 2 to 1, as is shown by this report from a HEISLER owner in Montana:

"Our HEISLER handles 30 cars where our saddle tank engine handles only 15 cars, and the HEISLER makes the same time from terminal to terminal and burns the same amount of fuel as the saddle tank with its lighter load." (Name and details on request.)

Another instance where the HEISLER has greatly outhauled the rod engine is found on the Bessemer Limestone & Cement Co. operations at Youngstown, Ohio. They report:

"Where the rod engine is hauling 8 loaded cars, the HEISLER hauls 12 to 15 — and is hauling its heavier loads where the rod engine would not dare to stick its nose."

Still another operator tells of the HEISLER'S extra hauling capacity. He writes:

"Where one of our 40-ton rod locomotives can haul 2 cars, our 36-ton HEISLER hauls three or four cars. And besides, the HEISLER

is the fastest engine on our work, because of its ability to get over rough track with ease." (Name and details on request.)

If you could take the time to visit a few of the big open-cut mining operations, quarries, construction jobs and logging operations where HEISLERS are used, you would get many more such reports of extra tonnage they have hauled with HEISLERS — and savings made in their hauling costs.

Cost records kept by these owners have shown very plainly that, to get the lowest cost per ton of material hauled, *you have to use the locomotive that costs least, per ton of hauling*, and per ton mile. Check the *cost* of different locomotives against their *hauling capacities*!

Find out the weight of trains pulled by HEISLERS, and by rod engines of the same weight, and you'll understand why the HEISLER'S *first cost is considerably lower, per ton of hauling capacity*.

Where HEISLERS are used, there is a smaller charge for direct locomotive costs on the tonnage hauled.

And besides, a lower charge per ton for wages of crews, because of fewer trips. Also less expense for track upkeep.

A 36-ton HEISLER, one of 9 owned by the Bessemer Limestone and Cement Co., hauling its regular train of three 20-yard cars and two 16-yard cars — a total weight of 217 tons hauled against a 3% grade with a 15 degree curve; considerably above its guaranteed capacity.

A Class 80 HEISLER speeding up the switching and spotting of cars at an Eastern paper mill. On work like this, where there are practically no grades, the HEISLER has shown important economies in operating costs, due to its greater power and 20% to 25% faster pick-up.

"..splendid locomotive for general service"

For switching cars and for all-around industrial hauling, users have found the HEISLER unequalled. And one operator (name on request) writes:

"Our HEISLER Locomotive has proven satisfactory for our switching— it is a decided improvement over the side rod locomotive of approximately the same weight which was formerly used."

On a 5½% grade— the HEISLER going up with two 30-yard cars of overburden—

And here you see the rod engine on the same 5½% grade shown in the photo above, bringing up one loaded car. (Details on request).

On this stripping job a 28-ton HEISLER easily started 8 cars of 12 tons each loaded, on a 5½% grade— while the 18-ton rod engine had to back into the pit and get a start to bring out four cars. The HEISLER is not as hard on the track as the lighter rod engine. (Name and details on request).

Besides cutting hauling costs, you increase output and reduce loading costs

By hauling a bigger tonnage per trip you eliminate much of the idle time of your shovels by making fewer switches of loads out and empties in. Figure out what this means in dollars and cents in your actual cost per yard or ton.

On one large earth moving job, two 55-ton HEISLERS hauling four 30-yard cars per trip on a four mile haul were able to replace three 63-ton rod engines hauling three cars per trip. It isn't hard to figure the savings in yardage and hauling costs on such a set-up.

Another important point to remember is that the HEISLER, with its quicker acceleration, spots your cars more quickly and accurately, resulting in less time lost per car when the trip is under the shovel.

As the general manager of a well-known company in Eastern Pennsylvania writes:

"Our 40-ton HEISLER has gone beyond our expectations—without in any way forcing this locomotive, we have been able to obtain a bigger output in less time, at a considerable saving in fuel."—(Name and details on request.)

When production must be pushed the HEISLER'S extra capacity is most appreciated.

The HEISLER'S extra capacity is something that you can *definitely depend on*, as it is put on your work with the guarantee to move at

A 42-ton HEISLER hauling six 30-ton capacity coal cars and two 12-yard dump cars, on Sherwood-Templeton Coal Company's stripping.

least 30% more material, ton per ton of locomotive, than a rod engine—hauling at the speed you require.

We'll be glad to help you figure how the extra hauling capacity of the HEISLER can be used to make larger profits on your work. No obligation on your part to get the facts.

Class 90 HEISLER, weighing 110 tons working order, on the Copper Queen Branch of the Phelps Dodge Corporation, Bisbee, Ariz. This HEISLER hauls 10 cars loaded with copper ore, weighing 640 tons, on a 2% grade and 30 degree curves.

This 55-ton HEISLER is hauling four heavily loaded 30-yard cars on a grade slightly steeper than 3%. Two HEISLERS, on trips of four miles to dump and return, keep a 4-yard electric shovel busy.

is what one operator recently wrote to another, who was considering the purchase of a locomotive:

"We have several sharp curves and about 400 ft. of 6% grades and the HEISLER hauls its heavier loads with ease."

This HEISLER hauls 13 heavily loaded 4-cubic yard cars full of shale on a 4% grade.

42-ton HEISLER owned by Northern Illinois Coal Corporation handling three cars weighing 30 tons empty —each car holding approximately 48 tons of coal. On this operation the grades vary from level to 4% against the load—exceeding 4% in some very short lengths. (See photo, Page 18.)

On grades, the HEISLER'S extra power
shows to most striking advantage

Most likely you have to haul against some steep grades— which present a serious hauling problem in many lines of industry.

In strip mining, logging, quarrying, and sand and gravel production, many grades have been found too difficult for an ordinary locomotive to negotiate economically.

When you have grades to contend with, you can overcome them by the means that have proven successful for other operators— easily pulling large trainloads with the powerful HEISLER.

In case after case where other engines had trouble in pulling *two* cars up a grade, HEISLERS of the same weight have gone in and pulled up *three or four cars*. Will be glad to give you full details.

The HEISLER shows to particular advantage in hauling up grades, because on steep hauls its smoother flow of power and greater wheel contact are of utmost importance.

Delivering greater power, in a smoother, steadier flow— with considerably more driving contact on the rails— it's only natural that

HEISLERS outpull heavier locomotives.

While our guarantee specifies that the HEISLER will haul at least 30% more than a rod engine of the same weight, many owners who are hauling on grades of 3% to 5%, or more, report that they are *getting 60% to 100% extra capacity*.

For instance, one user reports:

"Our HEISLER continues to give excellent satisfaction, hauling heavier loads than ever without any difficulty on grades approaching 7% to 8%."

And remember, even on very steep grades —some HEISLERS are operating on grades up to 13%— the HEISLER does not pull water. Its wagon-top boiler is especially designed to prevent the pulling of water while providing plenty of steam capacity for a long, hard grind.

To really appreciate the HEISLER, let us tell you where you can see them pulling heavy trains up steep grades. You'll be enthusiastic over the extra tonnage that you can move with this locomotive that *makes a specialty of the hardest work.*

On a 5½% grade this 42-ton HEISLER hauls two heavily loaded 30-yard cars

HEISLER Locomotive owned by Bond-Foley Lumber Co., Bond, Ky., handling train of logs on a 13% grade. (See letter at the left.)

"We have been using our HEISLERS over a switch-back for a number of years. They are powerful and well constructed—there seems to be no part of the HEISLER that gives any trouble.

"We can highly recommend the HEISLER to anyone needing a locomotive to pull heavy loads." F. V. Dabolt, Vice-President, Bond-Foley Lumber Co., Bond, Ky.

36-ton HEISLER hauling a 30-yard car, heavily loaded, up a $6\frac{1}{2}$% grade. J. Robert Bazley, Stripping Contr. Harleigh-Brookwood Coal Co., Morea, Pa.

75-ton HEISLER owned by the Coos Bay Lumber Co., Powers, Ore., hauling train of logs around curve and over trestle.

One of the four 42-ton HEISLERS at the West Clinton, Ind., operation of the Electric Shovel Coal Corporation, making its haul from pit to tipple.

HEISLER
GEARED LOCOMOTIVES

And on level track with easy grades, the HEISLER'S *extra capacity* and *speed* count

Even where your grades are not extreme, we put the HEISLER on your work with the guarantee to increase your hauling capacity at least 30%. The HEISLER doesn't have to operate on steep grades to show its extra hauling capacity—

But when hauling over smooth, well-ballasted track with easy grades, the greater power of the HEISLER is utilized for *extra speed*.

As one HEISLER owner, who is operating under such conditions, reports:

"Our 36-ton HEISLER makes better time on a 2½ mile run hauling 18 cars, than the 32-ton saddle tank with ten cars."

We can put you in touch with many owners whose HEISLERS are rendering double service— handling the long hauls over good track and rough track, and also switching and spotting on the short spurs.

The HEISLER is a real *double service* locomotive

It hauls much larger loads, with plenty of speed, over the long main-line hauls.

It speeds up your switching, and hauls far more over rough track.

The HEISLER fits in splendidly for *all-around* service, having shown its superiority for switching cars in every class of industrial hauling.

Since the HEISLER develops a much higher starting torque, picking up its loads 20% to 25% faster than a rod engine of the same weight, it spots cars just that much quicker.

When handling cars not equipped with brakes, the HEISLER stops them quicker and holds back a greater tonnage on a down grade. Better braking control is effected through the gear reduction against the cylinders and greater rail contact. The same principle as putting an automobile with four wheel brakes in gear, going down a long steep hill.

The same smooth flow of power that makes the HEISLER a faster starting engine, also gives much smoother stopping. When the load is thrown against the engine, the wheels do not have the same tendency to slip.

One of the two HEISLERS owned by the Oval Wood Dish Corp., Tupper Lake, N. Y. They write:
"We have had experience with other makes of locomotives, and we prefer the HEISLER."

HEISLER hauling loaded dump cars for grading. The HEISLER is geared right for heavy hauling— delivering at least 30% more power than a rod engine of the same weight, on level hauls or steep grades.

36-ton HEISLER hauling its regular train of three 20-yd. cars and two 16-yd. cars—working on a 3% grade with a 16 degree curve.

"Best engine to operate on sharp curves"

"It has been our experience that the HEISLER will stay with the track, and go where other locomotives cannot go. Because of its ability to work on sharp curves, steep grades and rough track, we are partial to the HEISLER."—Elmer I. Stoddard, Pres. and Gen. Mgr., The Grande Ronde Lumber Co., Perry, Ore.

Working on a 3% grade with a 16 *degree curve*. This 36-ton HEISLER is hauling its regular train of three 20-yard cars and two 16-yard cars—a total weight of 217 tons. Another case where the HEISLER is hauling beyond its guarantee.

Hauling timber cars for Snow Storm Silver Lead Co., Troy, Montana. The flexible action of the HEISLER'S free-swiveling trucks enables it to haul around very sharp curves—for instance a 65-ton HEISLER will negotiate a *50-foot radius* curve.

Hauling clay from bank to mill, Lock Haven Fire Brick Co., Lock Haven, Pa. Sharp curves like this are easily taken by the HEISLER, because of its free-swiveling trucks.

3½% grade with 22 degree curve, equal to a 4.5% grade on straight track. Here the extra hauling power of the HEISLER means the hauling of an extra 30-yard car each trip, and a big saving in hauling costs.

HEISLER
GEARED LOCOMOTIVES

Why the HEISLER takes sharp curves
without loss of power

Any user of locomotives who has had a wide experience with different makes, will tell you that the HEISLER has no equal for negotiating curves.

On industrial inter-plant hauling— on quarry and strip mine hauling— on logging operations— wherever you find extremely sharp curves, HEISLERS are taking them with ease where other locomotives have difficulty in running.

The reason is plain enough, when you make comparisons.

For instance, you find that a 24-ton HEISLER has a rigid wheel-base of *only* 44 *inches*, as compared with the 60-*inch* rigid wheel base of a 25-ton saddle tank engine.

That means a big difference in the radius of curve that each engine can take. *On standard gauge track, the 24-ton HEISLER can haul around a 40 foot radius curve*— where the 25-ton saddle-tank engine cannot even run.

And the HEISLER rounds a curve with its engine delivering *full power*— with practically no loss of power due to friction. The HEISLER'S free swiveling truck construction and short rigid wheel base allows every wheel to follow the curve with a minimum of binding at the flange.

Besides, there is very little slip at the drive shaft's Universal joint when rounding a sharp curve. As the drive shaft is central, its Universal joint can be set close to the center of pivot of each truck.

It's a revelation to most owners to watch their first HEISLERS haul heavy trains around sharp curves. As one owner reported:

Hauling "around a stump" for the Kent Lumber Co., Seattle, Wash.

"We are hauling heavy trains with our HEISLER around curves so sharp that a 12-yard dump car can barely stay on the rails."

Because of the HEISLER'S ability to take the sharp curves on woods track, loggers have a saying that "The HEISLER will run around a stump." And this ability of the HEISLER means a great deal on every class of hauling, as often it would be very expensive to lay track without sharp curves. Using the locomotive that takes sharp curves easily, without loss of power, can save you thousands of dollars in track laying cost, and track maintenance.

Your engine-men will soon find that they don't have to slow down to a "crawl" when rounding a curve or running over rough track with a HEISLER, as they would with a less flexible locomotive, or one having a higher center of gravity. The HEISLER is designed with a very low center of gravity, with its water tank behind the boiler instead of on top.

Don't hesitate to write us for further information about *what can be done on your own hauling*— we'll be glad to help you estimate the improvements a HEISLER will make.

The HEISLER takes sharper curves than any other locomotive of the same size, due to the much shorter wheel base of each truck.

"HEISLERS are very easy on track — we have much less trouble from surface kinking of rails, etc. Our pit tracks have many heavy curves, but the HEISLERS have no trouble negotiating them." — J. B. F. Melville, Vice-Pres., United Electric Coal Companies, Danville, Ill.

One of the HEISLERS used by "United Electric" at their Farmersburg stripping operation, hauling 12 cars on its regular run from pit to tipple. Read their report at the left, showing how the HEISLER keeps down track expense.

Sunlight Coal Co., 42-ton HEISLER on stripping work at Boonville, Ind. Hauling three 60-ton capacity cars out of the pit, working on grades of 3% to 4%.

36-ton HEISLER in Eastern Quarry.

This 36-ton HEISLER is one of nine HEISLERS used on a big earth moving job in Ohio.

HEISLER
GEARED LOCOMOTIVES

You save a lot of track expense
when you use HEISLERS

Because of the extremely flexible action of the HEISLER'S free-swiveling trucks, which do not "fight" the rails, there's far less wear and tear on the track.

You never see a HEISLER bouncing around on the rails, as you do locomotives with rigid wheel bases. The HEISLER rides any track smoothly, without bobbing around and jolting the rails out of alignment.

And there is no side-sway whatever— due to the HEISLER'S low center of gravity and perfect balance.

One place where you particularly notice the HEISLER'S saving of track maintenance is on the sharp curves, where any locomotive with a long rigid wheel base sets up heavy stresses that produce fast wear on track and tire flanges.

Another such place is where a locomotive is working back and forth over a single track. The HEISLER, being symmetrical and perfectly balanced over the center line, does not produce faster wearing of one rail.

With HEISLERS, owners can use lighter rails, and fewer ties spaced farther apart— important items for keeping down track expense.

For example, rail twice as heavy is needed for a 42-ton four-driver rod engine as for a 42-ton eight-driver HEISLER. Although the HEISLER has a much higher hauling capacity, it works safely on lighter rail because its weight is divided over eight drivers, and the power is applied more smoothly.

The HEISLER is practically as easy on track as the cars it pulls.

Naturally a car wears the rails less than the engine that is pulling it. A 50-ton car, for instance, is much easier on the track than an ordinary 35-ton engine, because of the driving force of the locomotive's wheels against the rails.

However, owners of HEISLERS will tell you that this engine, because of its smoother flow of power and equalization of power to all wheels, wears the track very little more than the cars it pulls.

You also save a good deal of expense in laying out track, when using the HEISLER. Less excavation is needed to keep down grades; less track shifting is needed to avoid sharp curves— as HEISLERS negotiate grades and curves more efficiently.

Just talk "track expense" to some owners of HEISLERS who have had experience with other locomotives, and you'll find that the savings made by the HEISLER on this item amount to real money. Drop us a line for some figures on this— records that you'll find interesting.

This 36-ton HEISLER is making its run from pit to tipple— hauling three cars of 100,000 lbs. capacity, a total of 216 tons up a grade of 4½%.

Another picture of the HEISLER on the Northern Illinois Coal Corporation stripping. Two loading shovels in tandem, and three locomotives hauling three-car trips, with a long haul, handle 3,000 tons in eight hours.

Unusually good record for low upkeep

"After working steadily every day for 1½ years the repair costs on our 65-ton HEISLER, exclusive of brake shoes, total only $35 —just about $22 a year."
—F. B. Snook, Supt., Dent's Run Railroad Company.

One of 10 HEISLERS employed on logging operations of Weyerhaeuser Timber Co.

32-ton, 48-inch gauge HEISLER handling four heavily loaded 10-yard dump cars on 4½% grade, for the Haddock Mining Co., Candlemas Collieries, Silverbrook, Pa. The 25-ton rod engine previously used on this grade handled only two cars.

HEISLER GEARED LOCOMOTIVES

The bigger hauled tonnage is obtained
with *far lower upkeep expense*

As you have been reading the many statements made by owners of HEISLERS, regarding the extra work these locomotives do, maybe you have asked the same question that another operator put up to us.

After watching a HEISLER hauling a big train-load, he said: "This certainly convinces me that the HEISLER has more hauling power than any other engine— but how much will it cost me to keep up a locomotive that is doing such strenuous work?"

To answer this question, we gave him some actual records showing how little it costs to operate a HEISLER in hard service. Here's one of the records we gave him:

Two 36-ton HEISLERS, in service 2½ years. Hauling five 16-yard air-dump cars against a grade, and working 10 hours a day right through the year (missing a few weeks in winter, but the time they double shifted more than made up the average to 10 hours a day for the 2½ years).

Total repair expense exclusive of brake shoes, for both these HEISLERS together for the 2½ years, was only $85— *an average of only $17 a year per locomotive.*

A remarkable record? Of course it is!— but we can show you others just about as good. For instance, that report sent in by Dent's Run Railroad— see Page 18.

The fact is that the HEISLER'S extra hauling power would mean little, if this locomotive did not have extra strength for the harder work it is called on to perform.

We fully realize how owners of HEISLER Locomotives are going to use them, when they find out what these locomotives will do. So we build the HEISLER with an extra margin of strength right through the machine.

Just inspect the HEISLER carefully, and you'll appreciate this. For example, note the construction of the HEISLER'S main frame, which is the "back-bone" of a locomotive. After you have sized up the rugged steel members of the main frame, which are a good deal heavier than seems necessary, remember this:

Even the HEISLERS which have met with severe abuse, such as no engine was ever intended to stand, show no evidence of rough treatment in the main frame. And breakage of a HEISLER'S main frame is practically unheard of.

The record of past years gives convincing proof of the more than ample strength provided by the HEISLER'S frame design.

And in every other part, down to the last detail, the HEISLER is built on this same plan— to stand years of hard work, giving *thoroughly dependable service year after year.*

The HEISLER easily starts and hauls fully loaded trains on temporary track against sharp curves and heavy grades. It has the extra strength to stand up year after year in this class of work.

One of seven HEISLERS used on stripping operations of Lehigh Navigation Coal Co. Photo shows 55-ton HEISLER handling train of four 30-yard dump cars—handled against stiff grades to dump.

36-ton HEISLER and 50-ton rod engine, both doing the same work—same number of cars on the same haul.

32-ton HEISLER in New York state stone quarry.

HEISLER
GEARED LOCOMOTIVES

On *every* class of heavy hauling, the HEISLER has shown its superiority

There are hundreds of companies using locomotives, who have, during the past few years, practically "tried them all."

They have tested every kind of locomotive —and, as you'll learn by making direct inquiries, the HEISLER Locomotive is now preferred by these experienced companies for their heavy hauling.

For such work as switching around the yards of industrial plants; hauling logs through the woods over rough spur track, and up steep switch-backs; pulling heavy trains of coal or ore from the steam shovels, in open-cut mining —in heavy hauling of every kind, the HEISLER has proven itself the ideal engine. *It is not equalled on such service.*

Besides being used very extensively in quarry hauling and coal stripping, you will find HEISLERS making big savings in haulage costs, and giving increased capacity, in various other industries. For example:

On heavy railroad construction

Hauling dirt and rock to the dump, or from borrow pit to fill, where it is necessary to move material fast, at low cost, and over temporary track.

As one well-known contractor, who has found what it means in extra profits to haul much bigger tonnage over rough track, sums up the HEISLER'S performance: "Only those who have seen HEISLERS in service can appreciate the real difference between the HEISLER and a rod engine."

In the chemical industry

Hauling limestone, ore, and other mineral deposits from open-pit mines and quarries; hauling logs from timber tracks; inter-plant hauls. Chemical manufacturers have found HEISLERS especially suited to their work.

In the words of J. D. Crosthwaite, Supt., McKean Chemical Co., Dahoga, Pa.:

"We are better pleased than ever with the HEISLER Locomotive, and now have two of them. Have used several other types of locomotives and the HEISLER is our choice."

Steel mill hauling

Steel men who have "tried them all" prefer the HEISLER for switching and spotting cars of coal, slag, ore, ingots, etc., and making up trains of finished products. In this work the HEISLER'S higher starting torque is a great advantage. And steel men also like the HEISLER'S ability to take sharper curves.

In logging service

On the West Coast, throughout the South, in fact wherever there are big timber operations, lumbermen depend on the HEISLER to get out their logs at minimum cost.

There are now hundreds of HEISLERS in logging service in all parts of the country, serving on the roughest woods hauling and also on main line hauls to the mill. Logging is a most severe test for a locomotive because rough track, sharp curves and steep grades are very common.

65-ton HEISLER owned by Dent's Run Railroad Co., hauling fifteen 100,000 lb. and 110,000 lb. capacity steel hopper cars. (Read what they say about the low cost of operating a HEISLER, Page 18.)

50-ton HEISLER of the Sunlight Coal Company, hauling seven 50-ton capacity cars—total weight approximately 500 tons. Working on 2¾% grade in combination with a sharp curve, from pit to storage yard. Hauling well above its guaranteed rating.

"The best investment we ever made"

"Our HEISLER has been in continual use since we purchased it, and in comparison with other locomotives we have had experience with, both geared and rod locomotives, would say that the HEISLER does twice as much work at half the upkeep expense."— A. G. McIntosh, Gen. Mgr., Native Lumber Co., Howison, Miss.

This HEISLER has encountered maximum grades up to 10%; has hauled as high as 1,700,000 ft. of logs in 12 months, over a five mile track. Owned by Sawyer-Goodman Lumber Co., Ontanogan, Mich.

42-ton HEISLER working on a grade with sharp curve, hauling beyond its rating.

The extra cars the HEISLER brings out of the pit make a considerable difference at the dump!

36-ton HEISLER owned by the Gayoso Lumber Co., of Memphis, Tenn. They write: "For the rated tonnage, we have found that the HEISLER handles 15% to 30% larger loads than any other type of locomotive."

Mechanical reasons back of
the HEISLER'S success

No other feature of locomotive design is more important than *balance*. A high margin of stability is necessary for safe operation on rough track, and *equal distribution of weight on all the drivers* is essential, to put the full power of the locomotive to work.

When you look over the modern HEISLER —the simplest and most rugged of geared locomotives— you'll see that its symmetrical design gives perfect balance.

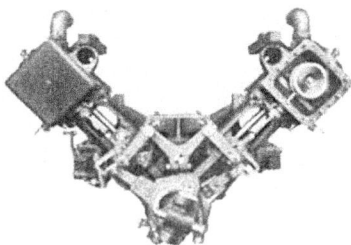

Perfect balance, with the V-type engines
on the center line.

The HEISLER has a V-type engine on the center line—supported by the main frame, entirely independent of the boiler.

One cylinder is on each side of the locomotive, and the connecting rods drive the central shaft *direct*.

Engine cylinders, piston rods, connecting rods and valve gear are all very easy to get at, but are out of the way of obstructions alongside or between the track.

The HEISLER'S center of gravity is very low, with the water tank behind the boiler. This, together with the perfectly symmetrical design, gives ideal *stability* for hauling around sharp curves and over rough track.

Power conserved by more simple transmission

The central driving shaft, to which the engine's connecting rods are direct-connected, is geared to one driving axle on each truck through a large bevel gear and pinion. *No friction loss due to needless gearing.*

Every wheel is a driver, one pair of wheels on each truck being turned by side rods. There are no trailing wheels on any HEISLER Locomotive— every pound of locomotive weight is utilized for traction.

The simple central driving shaft
of the HEISLER.
Note direct drive from crank shaft, and
position of universal joints.

The central position of the HEISLER'S driving shaft, with the boiler centered, also equalizes the load on different parts of the main frame, and greatly reduces strains on this important part, which is the backbone of a locomotive.

Hauling heavy log train on stiff grades and sharp curves, with HEISLER Locomotive equipped for burning oil.

"Spots cars accurately at the loading shovel —on any grade

"There is little or no tendency to skid when brakes are applied on the downgrade. With our HEISLER it is easy to start a train from a dead stop, up to the load limit."— (Write for the name of this operator, one of whose ten HEISLERS is shown in the photo above.)

36-ton HEISLER stripping for the Black Foot Coal Co., Oakland City, Ind. Has shown a very low operating cost.

65-ton HEISLER hauling 13 steel hopper cars for Dent's Run Railroad Company. Read their report on Page 18.

HEISLERS in steel plant service. In many places where a rod engine cannot run, HEISLERS are pulling their larger loads easily. Plenty of clearance on sharp curves, passing buildings, etc.

HEISLER GEARED LOCOMOTIVES

Swiveling trucks hold every wheel in contact with the rail

The hardest problem in designing the trucks of a heavy-hauling locomotive is to combine the perfect *flexibility* that holds every wheel in contact with rough temporary tracks, with the Ruggedness, Dependability and Low Upkeep of a rigid frame.

This combination has been worked out with splendid success in the HEISLER truck frame:

A patented 3-way swivel— perfectly flexible in its action, while rigid and sturdy in construction— holds each wheel in contact with the roughest track. Every wheel is always gripping the rail, carrying its full share of the locomotive's weight, and delivering its full share of the hauling power.

This equal distribution of the HEISLER'S weight permits the use of much lighter rails. When new track equipment is being bought,

a big saving can be made because of the lighter rail which can be used with the HEISLER— ties spaced farther apart, lighter trestles, etc.

When an 8-driver HEISLER is used in place of a 4-driver rod locomotive of the same weight it has been noted that the cost of track upkeep is cut down 40% to 50%.

Central drive-shaft delivers the power with neglible friction on the sharpest curves

As the HEISLER'S central driving shaft applies its power close to the center of the driving axles, the Universal coupling can be set very close to the center of pivot.

The coupling's telescopic slip, when rounding a sharp curve, is only 1/30 of what it would be if the power were applied at the end of the axle. Drive shaft friction is practically nothing on a HEISLER.

And the rigid wheel base of the HEISLER is shorter —a 32-ton HEISLER has only 44 inches of rigid wheel base and a 65-ton HEISLER only 66 inches. When pulling a heavy trainload around a curve, the HEISLER delivers its power as efficiently as on straight track— and we know of no other steam locomotive that will do this.

The central position of the driving gears also permits enclosing in a sturdy housing. The gears run in oil, fully protected from sand, grit, etc. Naturally gears with such protection last much longer. The gear cases also give protection in case of derailment, being strong enough to carry the weight of the locomotive. Such a thing as breakage of a HEISLER'S drive gears is practically unheard of.

Another HEISLER on construction work; hauls 8 or 9 of these cars. Contents of car, 24 tons; weight of car, 20 tons. Total trainload 352 tons. Working on 2½% grade.

"We are using our HEISLERS on heavier grades than originally planned, and getting very good service."— Lukens Steel Co., Coatesville, Pa.

36-ton, 36" gauge HEISLER hauling slag to the dump. It handles ingot cars, ladle cars, etc., for the Lukens Steel Co., Coatesville, Pa.

In Pennsylvania strippit; the HEISLER'S smooth flow of power gives a 20% to 25% quicker pick-up, and spots cars much faster.

The owners of this HEISLER report that it is speeding up the loading, and saving valuable steam shovel time.

HEISLER switching cars of coke, ore, billets, etc., at the blast furnace of an Eastern steel company.

HEISLER
GEARED LOCOMOTIVES

Geared *right* for heavy hauling

The HEISLER has a very much higher starting torque because the pistons of the HEISLER'S V-type engine make 2 to 2½ times as many strokes as a rod engine's per revolution of the driving wheels, giving the HEISLER a much smoother flow of power.

This is most important for heavy hauling, as the driving wheels do not have the same tendency to slip when starting a load.

And the higher starting torque of the HEISLER, besides giving a much smoother and quicker pick-up, affords exactly the same advantage for *deceleration*. The HEISLER'S gear ratio gives more than twice the braking action, when the power of the engine is thrown against the load — with the HEISLER'S drivers providing two or three times as much braking surface.

Boiler that delivers plenty of steam— and *no water*—for the steepest grade

The first haul your HEISLER makes up a long steep grade will convince you of the importance of the *over-capacity* of its free-steaming boiler.

This fast, economical steamer, that has shown 25% to 30% fuel savings, has plenty of capacity for the long, hard haul and *doesn't pull water* on the steepest grade. Every HEISLER has a boiler of extended wagon-top design.

The boiler is rigidly supported at the front end, and rests on a sliding bearing at the fire box, allowing free expansion. Can be taken off the main frame at any time without disturbing anything else but the cab and piping.

Every HEISLER boiler is thoroughly insulated with non-conducting lagging, then covered with a heavy steel jacket. Fire-box and grates are equipped for burning all kinds of coal, wood, or oil.

Ample tank capacity for fuel and water. Either a substantial coal bunker or wood rack is provided. When oil fuel is used, the oil tank is located above the water tank.

Besides the well-known HEISLER features which have been proven in service for many years, the latest HEISLERS are equipped with every modern device that increases hauling power.

For instance, super-heaters on HEISLERS have shown remarkable economy — and piston valves are used with super-heaters. Besides, the HEISLERS of today are being equipped with feed-water heaters, which have shown good economy.

And if you have "bad water"— water that has given trouble with any kind of steam equipment in the past— we can furnish your HEISLER with the modern "Filtrator" that gives you absolute protection from boiler scale, pitting, and corrosion.

This modern device has practically put an end to the problem of boiler upkeep expense, where water conditions have previously made it troublesome to use steam equipment.

Coming over a stiff grade with quite a sharp curve, this HEISLER is hauling its heavier load with ease.

HEISLER starting for the slag dump, Lukens Steel Co. Steel men find that they can move more material with this locomotive— haul more to the slag dump— switch and spot their cars faster.

"100% satisfactory"—

"We are pleased to state that the HEISLER is a wonderful engine when it comes to pulling heavy loads over rough tracks with low joints."—Crow Creek Gravel Co., Madison, Ark.

One of two HEISLERS owned by the Sherwood-Templeton Coal Company, operating at their Friar Tuck Mine near Linton, Indiana. This 42-ton HEISLER is hauling five 30-yard drop-bottom cars.

Another of the Electric Shovel Coal Corporation's HEISLERS working on the stripping at Staunton, Indiana.

West Fork Logging Company, Mineral, Wash., class 90 HEISLER, weighing 110 tons in working order, hauling heavily loaded log train up a steep grade with very sharp curve.

HEISLER
GEARED LOCOMOTIVES

Complete lubrication system assures smoother operation at all speeds

Another important feature of the HEISLER that you'll like, is the easy lubrication of all the principal bearings from *inside the cab*. Independent oil lines and positive force feed lubrication enable the operator to keep the bearings supplied with the right amount of lubricant.

Bearings which do not require frequent lubrication are reached by oil lines that run from either side of the locomotive—it is never necessary for the operator to go beneath the locomotive to lubricate.

All driving gears run in a constant bath of oil. The operator only needs to look at the oil level occasionally, to assure smooth operation of this powerful locomotive.

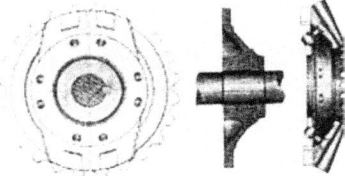

The Gears are rigidly clamped to the driving axles, the gear sectors engaging a cone that forms gear hub. Heavy lugs take the shearing strains, bolts serving only to hold the gear section in place.

ALL PARTS EASY TO GET AT. Adjustments and repairs to a HEISLER are comparatively few and far between, but when needed, are easily made without the use of pits or extensive shop facilities. All wearing parts are easily accessible for inspection.

Important bearings are of phosphor bronze or babbit-lined bronze for long dependable service—easily renewable.

Every HEISLER Locomotive is shipped equipped with a strong steel cab, complete auxiliary equipment, a full set of working tools and supplies, so that it may be put into service immediately upon arrival.

Replacing any worn part is a simple matter, as all parts are made to jigs, absolutely interchangeable. A complete stock of replacement parts is carried for immediate shipment.

The service that you get on parts is right up to the HEISLER standard of hauling service delivered by the HEISLER Locomotive. As W. P. Brown & Sons Lumber Co., Inc., Louisville, Ky., puts it:

"We have operated our HEISLER for a period of 14 months without ever having a wheel off the track. And another very satisfactory thing about using the HEISLER Locomotive is the excellent quick service given in shipping parts. We do not remember being delayed on any part ordered for our HEISLERS."

One of the HEISLERS used by "United Electric" at their Farmersburg stripping operation, hauling 12 cars on its regular run from pit to tipple. And they report that the HEISLER "fills the bill" for them 100%.

These tables do not give the *full* hauling capacity of HEISLER Locomotives

HEISLER Two-Truck Locomotive: Class Nos. 24-8-30 to 42-8-33 inclusive. 8 drivers.

THE figures given on the page opposite do not represent the full tonnage the HEISLER will haul— but these are approximately the loads that our haulage guarantee will be based on.

HEISLER Two-Truck Locomotive; Class Nos. 50-8-36 to 65-8-40 inclusive. 8 drivers.

HEISLER Three-truck Locomotive; Class Nos. 70-12-36 to 90-12-40 inclusive. 12 drivers.

There's a HEISLER that's just right for your work

Tell us about your hauling conditions, and we will help you estimate the improvements that you can depend upon with the HEISLER.

Descriptive folders, giving detailed data on the construction of three different classes of HEISLERS shown on this page, will be sent on request.

Also we'll gladly furnish prices and data on HEISLER Gas-Electric and Diesel-Electric Locomotives. Write us.

Heisler Locomotive Works Erie, Pa.

THE capacities are consistently *under* what many HEISLERS are doing in every day service.

The table figures cannot be taken as exact, because different conditions are met on every operation. However, these figures give you an idea of what you can depend on a HEISLER to haul, even when conditions are far from ideal.

Drop us a line regarding your particular conditions, and we will submit definite figures.

Will also be glad to send folders describing in detail the sturdy, simple, well balanced construction of HEISLER locomotives.

PLEASE compare these table figures, not with any other printed tables, but with the loads that other engines are *actually hauling*. This is necessary because the figures below do not represent optimistic claims made for the HEISLER— but what the HEISLER will actually equal or better.

Class Numbers and Capacities of HEISLER Geared Locomotives

Class	24-8-30	28-8-30	32-8-30	36-8-33	42-8-33	50-8-36	55-8-38	65-8-40	70-12-36	80-12-38	90-12-40
Code Word for Size of Locomotive	Argil	Arian	Arithmetic	Armill	Arouse	Arsenal	Artful	Ascend	Ascribe	Ashes	Aside
Weight in average working order—Lbs.	48000	56000	64000	72000	84000	100000	110000	130000	162000	177000	198000
Weight in full working order—Lbs.	55000	62000	70000	79000	92000	109000	121000	143000	181000	196000	219000
2-Cylinders— Dia. and Stroke	11″x10″	12″x10″	12½″x12″	13″x12″	14″x12″	15″x12″	15½″x14″	16¾″x14″	16¾″x14″	17¼″x15″	18¼″x16″
Number of Driving Wheels	8	8	8	8	8	8	8	8	12	12	12
Diameter— Driving Wheels	30″	30″	30″	33″	33″	36″	38″	40″	36″	38″	40″
Rigid Wheel Base	44″	44″	44″	50″	56″	56″	61″	66″	66″	61″	66″
Total Wheel Base	20′- 0″	21′- 0″	21′- 4″	23′- 6″	25′-0″	25′-11″	27′- 1″	30′- 0″	39′-0″	40′- 6″	44′-10″
Total Length Over All	28′- 8″	29′-10″	30′- 4″	32′- 0″	33′-5″	36′- 3″	38′- 6″	41′- 0″	49′-4″	50′- 5″	55′-10″
Extreme Height Above Rail	10′- 3″	10′- 4″	10′-10″	10′-11″	11′-3″	11′- 3″	11′-10″	12′- 6″	12′-4″	12′-6″	12′-10″
Extreme Width	7′-11″	7′-11″	8′-11″	8′-11″	9′-5″	9′- 6″	9′-11″	9′-11″	10′-3″	10′-3″	10′-10″
Capacity— Water in gallons	750	925	1075	1250	1375	1600	1800	2150	3430	3430	4000
" — Coal in pounds	2700	3000	4000	4100	5000	6000	7300	8500	10600	10600	11500
" — Wood in cords	1	1¼	1½	1½	1½	1½	2	2½	3	3	3½
" — Oil in gallons	310	340	450	450	500	680	716	905	1280	1280	1350
Sharpest Advisable Curve—Radius	40′	40′	40′	40′	40′	50′	50′	50′	100′	100′	100′
Advisable weight of Rail—Lbs. per Yd.	25	30	30	35	40	45	50	60	50	50	60
Minimum Weight of Rail—Lbs. per Yd.	20	25	25	30	35	40	45	55	45	45	55
Working Pressure—Lbs.	175	175	175	190	190	200	200	200	200	200	200
Minimum Practical Gauge— Inches	24″	24″	30″	30″	36″	36″	36″	36″	36″	56½″	56½″
Tractive Force—Lbs. calculated at 75% of boiler working pressure	12350	14890	17200	18970	22000	24375	26550	32130	35460	38480	43600
Tractive Force—Lbs. calculated at 85% of boiler working pressure	13990	16870	19490	21500	24920	27620	30090	36410	40180	43610	49410

Hauling capacities in tons, of 2000 pounds, exclusive of locomotive, based upon tractive power at 75% OF BOILER WORKING PRESSURE, 8 pounds per train ton rolling friction and straight track.

On Absolutely Level Straight Track.	1520	1833	2118	2335	2708	2997	3264	3951	4352	4722	5351
" 1% Grade 52.8 Ft. per Mile	417	504	582	641	744	821	893	1082	1185	1286	1458
" 2% " 105.6 " " "	233	282	326	359	416	458	498	604	658	714	809
" 3% " 158.4 " " "	158	191	221	243	282	308	335	407	440	478	542
" 4% " 211.2 " " "	116	141	163	180	208	227	247	300	322	349	396
" 5% " 264.0 " " "	90	110	127	140	162	176	191	232	247	258	305
" 6% " 316.8 " " "	72	88	102	112	130	140	152	186	196	213	242
" 7% " 369.6 " " "	59	73	84	92	107	115	124	152	159	172	196
" 8% " 422.4 " " "	50	61	70	77	89	95	103	126	130	140	161
" 9% " 475.2 " " "	42	51	59	65	75	80	86	104	108	117	133
" 10% " 528.0 " " "	35	44	51	55	64	67	73	87	89	97	111

The hauling capacity of locomotives is based upon tractive force, rolling friction, grade resistance and curve resistance. Under conditions of rough and uneven track the ability of a locomotive to utilize all of its tractive force has a very great bearing upon hauling capacity. The flexible construction of the HEISLER Locomotive insures maximum hauling capacity.

Rolling friction varies considerably with the condition of track, weight per axle, lubrication and kind of cars, etc. For average conditions 8 to 12 pounds per train ton may be figured. With heavy, well lubricated cars and extra good track 6½ lbs. may be figured. With poor track and cars it is often 20 lbs. or more and for mine cars in bad condition, may run as high as 60 lbs. Grade resistance is exactly 20 lbs. per train ton for each per cent of grade, while curve resistance may be figured at 0.8 lbs. per train ton for each degree of curvature.

The following example shows how to find the size locomotive needed for certain conditions: What size locomotive would be required to haul 300 tons over a 2 per cent grade and 25 degree curve, figuring rolling friction at 8 lbs. per train ton?

It will be seen that the resistance to be overcome is 2 x 20, + 0.8 x 25, + 8 or 68 pounds per train ton. Multiplying 300 by 68=20400, the total train resistance.

Now suppose a Class 50-8-36 HEISLER weighing 50 tons in average working order for this work. Multiplying 50 by 68=3400, total engine resistance.

Adding 20400, the train resistance and 3400, the locomotive resistance, we have a total resistance of 23800 pounds to be overcome. The tractive force of the locomotive is 24375 lbs.; it will therefore handle the load under the above conditions.

Note: Tractive power of rod locomotives is regularly calculated at 85% of boiler working pressure

Due to the higher torque and more uniform turning movement of a geared locomotive higher tractive power, per ton of locomotive weight, may be utilized without slipping the driving wheels. It should be borne in mind that the increased hauling capacity of the HEISLER is due not only to its higher tractive power, but also to its *more uniform* flow of power and other features that you have read in preceding pages.

Curves— Simple way to designate

The simplest way of designating a railroad curve is to give the length of the radius—*i. e.*, the distance from the center to the outside of the circle, or one-half the diameter. The shorter the radius, the sharper the curve. The length of the radius is usually stated in feet. The length of the radius of a railroad curve is measured to the center of the track.

Degree and Radius of Curves

Degree	Radius in Feet	Degree	Radius in Feet	Degree	Radius in Feet
1	5730	26	220	51	112
2	2865	27	212	52	110
3	1910	28	206	53	108
4	1432	29	197	54	106
5	1146	30	191	55	104
6	955	31	185	56	102
7	818	32	179	57	100
8	716	33	174	58	98.9
9	636	34	169	59	97
10	573	35	163	60	95.5
11	521	36	159	61	94
12	477	37	155	62	92
13	441	38	150	63	90.9
14	409	39	147	64	89.5
15	382	40	143	65	88
16	358	41	139	66	86.8
17	337	42	136	67	85.5
18	318	43	133	68	85
19	301	44	130	69	83
20	286	45	127	70	81.8
21	273	46	125	71	80.7
22	260	47	122	72	79.5
23	249	48	119	73	78
24	238	49	117	74	77
25	229	50	114	75	76

Method of designating grades

Proportional	Percent	Feet per mile
¼ in 100	¼ of 1	13.2
½ " 100	½ of 1	26.4
¾ " 100	¾ of 1	39.6
1 " 100	1	52.8
1½ " 100	1½	79.2
2 " 100	2	105.6
2½ " 100	2½	132
3 " 100	3	158.4
3½ " 100	3½	184.8
4 " 100	4	211.2
4½ " 100	4½	237.6
5 " 100	5	264
5½ " 100	5½	290.4
6 " 100	6	316.8
6½ " 100	6½	343.2
7 " 100	7	369.6
7½ " 100	7½	396
8 " 100	8	422.4
8½ " 100	8½	448.8
9 " 100	9	475.2
9½ " 100	9½	501.6
10 " 100	10	528
. . . .	. . . .	. . . .
. . . .	. . . .	. . . .
. . . .	. . . .	. . . .

Rule for measuring the radius of a sharp curve

Stretch a string, say twenty feet long, or longer if the curve is not a sharp one, across the curve corresponding to the line from A to C in the diagram.

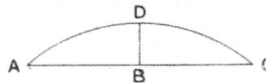

Then measure from B, the center of the line AC, and at right angles with it to the rail at D.

Multiply the distance A to B, or one-half the length of the string in inches, by itself; measure the distance from D to B in inches and multiply it by itself. Add these two products and divide the sum by twice the distance from B to D, measured exactly in inches and fractional parts of inches. This will give the radius of the curve in inches.

It may be more convenient to use a straight-edge instead of a string. Care must be taken to have the ends of the string or straight-edge touch the same part of the rail as is taken in measuring the distance from the center. If the string touches the bottom of the rail flange at each end, and the center measurement is made to the rail head, the result will not be correct.

Example—Let AC be a 20-foot string; half the distance of AB is then 10 feet, or 120 inches. Suppose BD is found on measurement to be 3 inches. Then 120 multiplied by 120 is 14,400, and 3 multiplied by 3 is 9; 14,400 added to 9 is 14,409, which, divided by twice 3, or 6, equals 2401½ inches, or 200 feet 1½ inches, which is the radius of the curve.

The formula is stated: $\dfrac{AB^2 + BD^2}{2BD} = R$. Or, applied to the above example: $\dfrac{120^2 + 3^2}{2 \times 3} = 2,401\tfrac{1}{2} = 200$ feet, 1½ inches.

To find the size of rail needed

Multiply the number of tons (of 2,000 pounds) on one driving wheel by eight, and the result is the number of pounds per yard of the lightest rail advisable. This rule is only approximate, and is subject to modification in practice.

Note— If, as is often the case with four-wheel direct connected locomotives, the weight on front and back driving wheels is not the same, the heavier weight must be taken.

Easy method of measuring heavy grades

Of course, the proper way of determining grades is by surveyor's instruments. But where the grade varies many times in a distance of a few hundred feet, it is quite as important to know the maximum as the average grade. In such cases it is sufficiently accurate to use a straight-edge 100 inches long, and, leveling it with an ordinary spirit level, to measure in inches from bottom of straight-edge to top of rail. This gives the grade in per cent, which can be reduced to feet per mile by multiplying by 52.8. A few trials in different places will readily determine the ruling grades. On very low grades this method is not practicable, but it is useful on most of the roads where our special-service engines are running, the grades varying from 1 to 10 per 100.

HEISLER LOCOMOTIVE WORKS, Erie, Pa., U. S. A.

The New York Subway
ITS CONSTRUCTION AND EQUIPMENT

INTERBOROUGH
RAPID
TRANSIT
-1904-

Reprinted by PeriscopeFilm.com

On October 27, 1904, the Interborough Rapid Transit Company opened the first subway in New York City. Running between City Hall and 145th Street at Broadway, the line was greeted with enthusiasm and, in some circles, trepidation. Created under the supervision of Chief Engineer S.L.F. Deyo, the arrival of the IRT foreshadowed the end of the "elevated" transit era on the island of Manhattan. The subway proved such a success that the IRT Co. soon achieved a monopoly on New York public transit. In 1940 the IRT and its rival the BMT were taken over by the City of New York. Today, the IRT subway lines still exist, primarily in Manhattan where they are operated as the "A Division" of the subway. Reprinted here is a special book created by the IRT, recounting the design and construction of the fledgling subway system. Originally created in 1904, it presents the IRT story with a flourish, and with numerous fascinating illustrations and rare photographs.

Originally written in the late 1900's and then periodically revised, A History of the Baldwin Locomotive Works chronicles the origins and growth of one of America's greatest industrial-era corporations. Founded in the early 1830's by Philadelphia jeweler Matthais Baldwin, the company built a huge number of steam locomotives before ceasing production in 1949. These included the 4-4-0 American type, 2-8-2 Mikado and 2-8-0 Consolidation. Hit hard by the loss of the steam engine market, Baldwin soldiered on for a brief while, producing electric and diesel engines. General Electric's dominance of the market proved too much, and Baldwin finally closed its doors in 1956. By that time over 70,500 Baldwin locomotives had been produced. This high quality reprint of the official company history dates from 1920. The book has been slightly reformatted, but care has been taken to preserve the integrity of the text.

NOW AVAILABLE AT
WWW.PERISCOPEFILM.COM

A HISTORY OF THE
BALDWIN
LOCOMOTIVE
WORKS
1831-1920

Reprinted by PeriscopeFilm.com

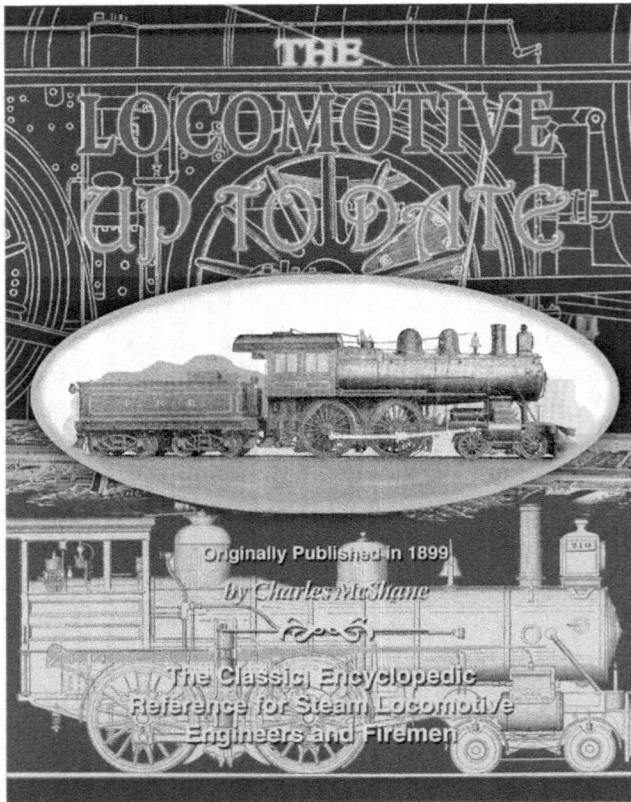

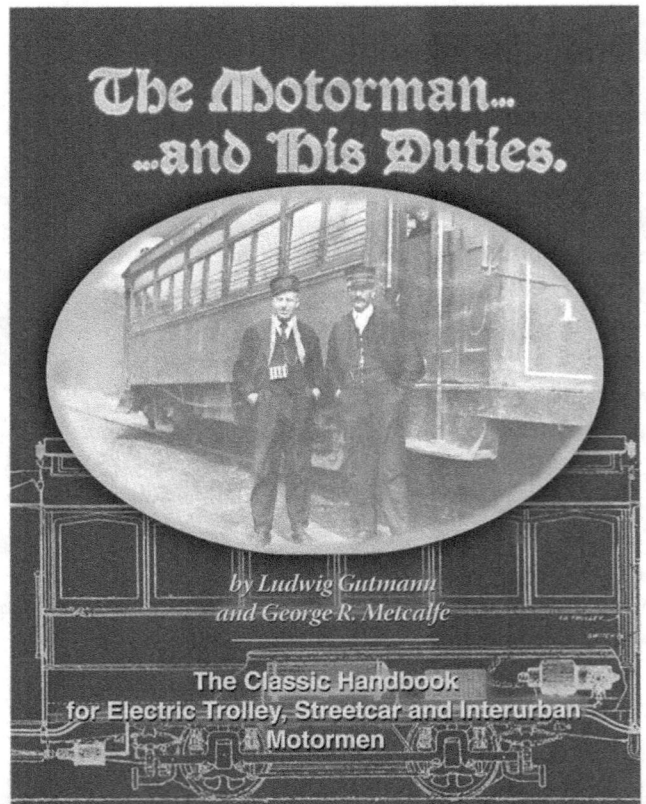

www.ingramcontent.com/pod-product-compliance
Lightning Source LLC
LaVergne TN
LVHW081326060426
835511LV00011B/1887